CONTENTS

CHAPTER 1

UNDERSTANDING QUIET

>>>>>>>>

You arrive at a party at your classmate's house, but your good friend isn't there yet. You only recognize a few faces. You see people you've met a few times and others who are complete strangers. You're not quite sure where to stand or who to talk to. You start feeling hot and fidgety. What do you do?

The idea of going to a party can make some people uncomfortable, especially if there will only be a few people they know there. Some people may feel nervous when meeting new people and making new friends. They don't know what to say or how to act. It's a feeling that a lot of people know well.

Do you ever feel this way? Maybe you're afraid that others might not like you. Do you think you'll say or do the wrong thing? Maybe you simply feel drained when you're in places with a lot going on. Those feelings can prevent you from talking to others or spending a lot of time in social situations. If you feel this way, it's okay. It happens to a lot of people. But that doesn't mean you can't go out and make new friends. There's a wonderful friend inside you who wants to connect with others. You don't need to be the loudest, funniest person to feel good in social situations. You just need to find the ways of socializing that work for you.

WHY ARE YOU QUIET?

Everyone is quiet for different reasons. It can be helpful to understand the different reasons that make people who they are.

You may be shy or introverted. You also may be a little of both. If you are shy, you might be afraid of talking to other people. Introverted people feel drained if they are around others for too long. They shut down and need time alone before being sociable again. Don't worry too much about why you are quiet. Focus on accepting who you are and understand that you don't need to change to be a great friend to others.

Social anxiety

Some people have social anxiety. Social anxiety is an extreme fear of social situations. This fear may cause people to avoid going to parties or other events. If you think you have anxiety or another mental health disorder that affects your everyday life, ask for help. Tell a trusted adult. An adult can help connect you with a counsellor or doctor. Page 46 also has resources that can help you.

SHY GUIDES

GETTING OUT AND GETTING ALONG

The Shy Guide to Making Friends and Building Relationships

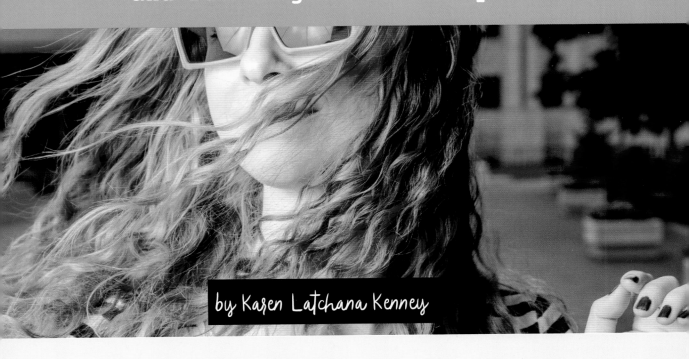

by Karen Latchana Kenney

raintree

a Capstone company — publishers for children

Raintree is an imprint of Capstone Global Library Limited, a company incorporated in England and Wales having its registered office at 264 Banbury Road, Oxford, OX2 7DY – Registered company number: 6695582

www.raintree.co.uk
myorders@raintree.co.uk

Edited by Abby Colich
Designed by Kay Fraser
Picture research by Morgan Walters
Production by Laura Manthe
Originated by Capstone Global Library
Printed and bound in India

ISBN 978 1 4747 6805 4
23 22 21 20 19
10 9 8 7 6 5 4 3 2 1

British Library Cataloguing in Publication Data
A full catalogue record for this book is available from the British Library.

Acknowledgements
We would like to thank the following for permission to reproduce photographs: Shutterstock: Asia Images Group, 41, Cookie Studio, 17, CREATISTA, 37, Daisy Daisy, 42, Daniel M Ernst, 26, 31, Dean Drobot, 6, 47, Diana Grytsku, 43, Elena Elisseeva, 34, Featureflash Photo Agency, bottom 15, Flamingo Images, 11, gpointstudio, 33, Iakov Filimonov, 18, 23, Imagincy, 20, Just2shutter, 16, Leonard Zhukovsky, bottom 9, LightField Studios, 24, Mettus, Cover, 1, Monkey Business Images, 5, 13, 19, pixelheadphoto digitalskillet, 45, PrinceOfLove, top 9, Rawpixel.com, 3, 7, 27, 28, s_bukley, bottom 21, Samuel Borges Photography, top 21, wavebreakmedia, 38, WindNight, top 15

Every effort has been made to contact copyright holders of material reproduced in this book. Any omissions will be rectified in subsequent printings if notice is given to the publisher.

We would like to thank Christopher A. Flessner, PhD., Associate Professor, Department of Psychological Sciences and Director, Pediatric Anxiety Research Clinic (PARC) at Kent State University, Ohio, USA, for his help in the preparation of this book.

>>> QUIZ: WHAT'S YOUR PERSONALITY?

Take this quiz to find out more about who you are. Answer yes or no to each question.

1. Do you like hanging out with a few friends more than a large group?

2. Are you a great listener?

3. Do you take the time to think before you speak?

4. After hanging out with your friends for a while, do you start to feel tired or drained?

5. Do you feel tense and stiff around people you don't know very well?

6. Do you sometimes have trouble thinking of things to say?

If you mostly answered "yes", you're probably a more shy or introverted person. Being around other people may drain you of energy. If you answered "no" to most of the questions, you're more likely an extrovert. Being alone can be difficult for you. You get more energy being in social situations. Both personality types have lots of positive traits. Try to focus on your positive traits as you discover more about who you are and how you can thrive in social situations.

CHAPTER 2

FROM ALONE TIME TO FRIEND TIME

>>>>>>>>

What's your idea of the perfect afternoon? Does it involve a book and a beanbag? Perhaps you like playing video games during your free time. Or maybe you like going on long bike rides. A lot of people value alone time. Being alone helps you relax and rest. Alone time might give you energy to go out and be sociable later. But if you spend too much time alone, you might start to feel lonely. Loving alone time doesn't mean that you don't want friends. You just need to balance it with some friend time too.

Everyone can make friends. Friends are important to have. They are the people you can say anything to. You can tell them your funniest jokes or act silly with them without feeling stupid. They're there for fun adventures and even when you're sad. You can rely on them, and they make life more exciting.

We all have different kinds of friends. Some friends are more like acquaintances. You know them, but not really well. Close friends are people you know well. You have built a strong relationship with them. Close friends might start out as acquaintances. But as you get to know them better, they can become your best friends. Some friends stay acquaintances, and that's okay. It doesn't matter how many friends or acquaintances you have. Knowing yourself and your likes will help you choose friends who are right for you.

Kevin Durant

US basketball star Kevin Durant called himself an introvert in an interview. But this has never held him back in sport. He gave credit to his coach and teammates for their part in having a successful basketball season. He says his coach told him not to worry about what other people say. His team embraced him for who he is and didn't try to change him. They wanted him to be himself.

Maybe you're not the kind of person who can walk into a group and join in on the conversation straight away. That's okay. You don't have to be that kind of person to make friends. We all make friends in different ways.

It helps to first know yourself and your strengths. You'll work out all the wonderful qualities you have to offer a friend. Ask people you know what they like about you or what they think you are good at. See if they can come up with at least three things. Enlist family members or a friend. It may surprise you what they say. What comes easily to you may be difficult for others. Pay attention and really listen. Sometimes it takes someone else's observations to help you understand yourself better.

Then look at your own observations about yourself. Think about what you really like to do and what you're really good at, and be honest. If you like building robots or learning obscure facts about bugs – be proud of it. Your interests make you who you are. Be proud of who you are, even if some of your interests aren't popular. Having confidence about what you like will attract other people. They'll want to know more about you.

LIFE TIP

Brainstorm a list of your interests and strengths. What are your favourite books, films and music? Write down what you're really good at and the things you care about, such as animals, football or painting.

>>> Know your strengths

You may have many strengths that others might not recognize straight away. Many quiet people are great at:

- listening carefully to others

- paying attention to details

- solving problems

- being loyal and caring friends

- motivating themselves to do things

- being creative

STARTING SMALL: FRIENDSHIP GOALS

Once you know more about who you are, you'll have a better idea about what you can offer a friend. But the goal of making new friends can still seem impossibly big. Where do you start?

Like with any big goal, you need to take small steps to get there. Friendships start small, but they need to start *somewhere*. Being friendly is one of the first keys to meeting someone new. Start with some simple goals:

- Say "hello" to someone in the corridor at school.

- Ask someone you don't know to be your partner for a class project.

- Talk to someone who is usually sitting alone at lunch.

- Offer to assist someone who looks like he or she needs help.

Try a new goal each day or week. You can even write down a list of goals. Cross them off as you accomplish them. On your first try, it might seem scary. But facing your fears will help you overcome them. Each goal will get a little easier the second or third try. Be patient with yourself. You're not going to be a pro right away, but you'll see these small goals adding up over time. You'll start meeting some new people. Meeting people is the first step in making new friends.

CHAPTER 3

>>>>>>>>>>>> # YOU ARE NOW LEAVING YOUR COMFORT ZONE

Do you sit in the same place in the canteen every day, next to the same people? Do you have an after-school routine that never changes – straight home for homework, snack and then reading? If you do the same things every day, you may be stuck in your comfort zone.

Your comfort zone is all the habits and actions you do every day that you've become used to. These habits and actions make you feel safe and comfortable. You know what to do and what to expect. It's perfectly normal to have a comfort zone – everyone has a comfort zone. But it's important to get out of it too.

Don't let your comfort zone limit what you do. Challenge yourself to try new things. Trying new things will help you grow as a person. With every new situation you are in, there will be new people to meet. That means more opportunities to make new friends.

LIFE TIP

Keep a journal of the things you do every day. Just make a short list. You'll start to see your patterns, and you might be surprised by what they are. But knowing them will help you change them.

>> Zendaya

ctress Zendaya is best known for her roles Shake It Up, The Greatest Showman and two pider-Man films. As a child, she was very shy. ven though she didn't want to, Zendaya's arents encouraged her to try performing. Once he was on stage, she loved it. All it took was for er to try something new just once.

MAKE THE CHANGE

Are you ready to leave your comfort zone? And where are you going? Take action to find new opportunities. Sign up for a class or a club at school that you wouldn't normally choose. In fact, pick something that's the opposite of what you always do. Try karate, chess club or the band. You may love it, and even if you don't, at least you'll have tried something new. If you do love an activity, you'll meet other people with a similar interest. That connection can help spark a friendship.

At first, try changing just one thing in your everyday routine. At lunch, sit at a different table. Talk to someone new. Ask someone in your class to hang out with you after school. Smile at someone you don't know.

As you become more confident outside of your comfort zone, try some more challenging activities. Host a small party. Invite some of the new people you've met. Keep it short and fun. Plan games you can play together. Your guests will all get to know one another a little better. You can also try joining some groups or classes that push you more into the spotlight, such as a debate club or an acting class. With each step, you'll learn more about yourself and meet other people who like to do the same things as you.

>>> 3 ways to break out of the zone

Try these ideas to get out of your comfort zone and connect with others.

1. Sign up for a pottery, photography, painting or other kind of artistic class. You'll express yourself and meet others interested in art too.

2. Find a book club. Book clubs bring together the quiet activity of reading with a social acivity. Pick a group that reads the kinds of books you like.

3. Put your hand up to answer some of your teacher's questions. If you know what the class is discussing that day, write down some thoughts before you go. It helps to have notes to look at. Your classmates will get to hear your thoughts and may learn more about you.

SMALL-TALK STARTERS

How do you start the small talk? First, you should be curious and interested in learning about others. What does the person you want to talk with seem to be interested in? Is she always reading comic books? Is he a maths whizz? Does she like to draw cats on pretty much *everything*? Pay attention and notice what the person likes before you start a conversation.

Start chatting by asking a question such as, "How did you work out that fraction so quickly?" Or give a compliment such as, "Nice comic book!" It shows you are interested in knowing more about that person.

Try to keep the small talk going. Listen to the person's answers. Make good eye contact while you're listening too. It shows you are paying attention. Add your thoughts and think of follow-up questions from that person's answers. You may find that you really have something in common. If you do, talk about it. And guess what? You've just taken a step from small talk into a deeper conversation!

Like most things, small talk takes some practice to master. It might seem awkward at first, but each attempt teaches you what works and what doesn't. If you're nervous, break it down. Ask yourself, *What's the worst thing that can happen?* You may not hit it off with one person, but there are plenty of other people you will connect with. After you try some small talk, think about what worked and what didn't. Build on what works and try again with someone new. Over time, you'll develop your own small-talk style.

Your go-to glossary of small-talk phrases

It may help to have some small-talk phrases on hand. If you are nervous and can't think of something to say, you can use one of them. Here are a few to try:

- *What did you do this weekend?* This is an open-ended question. It needs more than a "yes" or "no" answer. It'll probably get someone chatting.

- *What's your favourite part in that book?* This connects with someone's interest – books, films and more. They will be more likely to chat about something if they enjoy it.

- *Nice sweatshirt! So do you like sports club?* Notice a sports club logo on someone's sweatshirt? Give her a compliment about it. It will make her feel good. And it opens the door for more chitchat. She's wearing it for a reason. It says something about who she is.

- *Did you see the end of the game last night?* Do you like a certain sports team and know someone else does too? Or was there a game your whole town is talking about? Sports are a great way to start a conversation.

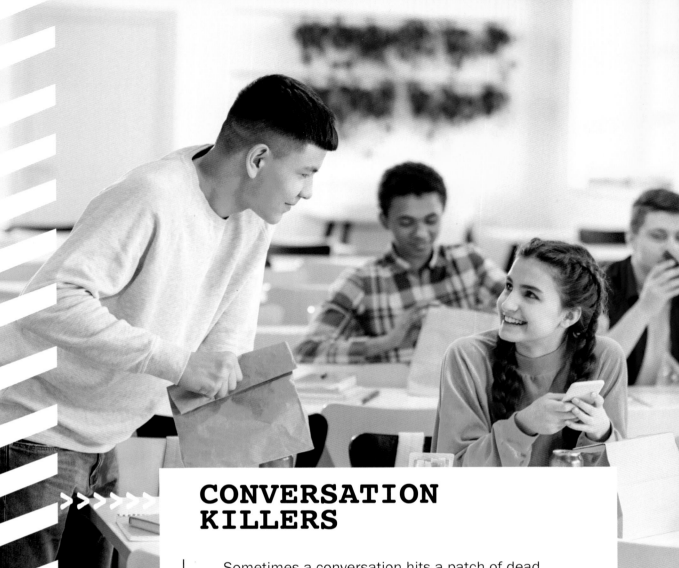

CONVERSATION KILLERS

Sometimes a conversation hits a patch of dead silence. It's awkward. It's quiet. What has happened?

You may have accidentally killed the conversation. Don't worry though! It happens to everyone. Did you just describe every detail about a wart on your foot? Or did you just say your friend looked really, really tired? Saying personal things like that can cut small talk short. Keep the conversation light if you can. It's probably best to save the personal stuff for deeper conversations with close friends.

Or maybe that silence has nothing to do with you at all. Your friend could be distracted or having a bad day. For example, your friend might seem anxious and keep looking at the time. He might have to be somewhere in five minutes but doesn't want to seem rude.

If you don't want the conversation to be over, try one of your go-to small-talk phrases. It might spark the conversation to continue. But don't push it. Pay attention to what your friend says and does. If it seems like he wants to get going or if you do, exit the conversation politely. You might say, "I need to get going." Or, "It was great seeing you!" Both work well. You can even add something about the next time you'll meet, like "See you in class!" It ends the conversation on a positive note.

TALKING IN GROUPS

Small talk is a great way to start a one-on-one conversation. But what if there's a group of people talking after school or football practice? You can use small talk to join in on a group discussion.

Don't be afraid of large groups. Yes, they can be loud. The topic may change quickly. It may seem like one person is doing all the talking. Knowing when to talk and how to be heard can be hard, but it is possible.

First, know that you're probably not going to be talking about something very deep. The conversation will probably be about a new TV show, a video game or some funny thing that happened that day. Pay attention to what other people are talking about. Then see if it's something you're interested in too.

If you're nervous, start with small phrases. Add little comments to show that you agree or understand. "Yeah, totally!" or "You're kidding!" or even "You're right!" Even a smile, chuckle, *um-hmmm* or nod adds to the conversation. It shows you're really listening and understanding what the other people are talking about.

If you have something to say, wait until there is a pause in the conversation. Make sure you speak in a voice that's loud enough to be heard. If you're too quiet, no one will be able to hear you. If you are interrupted, don't take it personally. It's just part of talking in a group.

CHOOSING THE RIGHT GROUP

Don't get caught up in whether or not you're joining the most popular group. Popularity isn't as important as it may seem. Not all people will be in the most popular groups. Look at everyone in your school as being possible friends – popular or not. Be inclusive, not exclusive.

Sometimes the group conversations, whether with popular people or not, can turn negative. People may gossip or complain. If this happens, don't add to the negativity. Try to make the conversation more positive to lighten it up. Try changing the subject. Ask if anyone else is nervous about the upcoming maths test. Or ask everyone what their plans are for the weekend.

Real friendships are based on common values and respect for each other. They're the kind that last. Some groups of friends could break up at any moment. Friendship based on bullying, gossip or other negativity and bad behaviour shouldn't have a place in your life. It's a fake kind of friendship that won't last. Keeping the conversations positive and constructive with your friends will help make your relationships healthy and strong.

>>>> What social media doesn't tell you

Social media can be a great way to connect with others. However, don't forget what others post isn't always real. Selfies in perfect lighting and posts showing people having fun don't always show the whole picture. Most people don't post pictures of themselves feeling lonely, having a bad day or doing unexciting things. Some users create an image of their lives in which everything looks great and exciting. Remember that and take some social media breaks. It will clear your head from the constant feeds.

FINDING YOUR CHARISMA

Once you've got the basics of individual and group conversation down, try adding to those. One way to do this is to find your charisma. Ever notice how some people seem to easily attract friends? Others feel good around them and just want to be near them. Having charisma means you show that you care about others. It doesn't mean you're overly excited about everything. That can seem fake and forced. Instead, let your own kind of charisma shine through.

So how do you develop charisma? First, really be *there* when you're talking to someone. Don't think about how much homework you have to do or where you need to be in an hour. Try not to fidget or look around. Just focus on your friend, right in that moment. Nod to show you're listening.

Then balance your interest in others with confidence in yourself. Show that you are relaxed and comfortable when conversing with others. If you're not sure what someone else is talking about, ask follow-up questions so that you understand better.

Focus on the positive too. You have a choice about how you think about every situation. Choose to be more positive in your thinking. Then share that positive attitude with others. Make positive comments to the people you talk with. They'll feel good about you and themselves after your conversation.

> Body talk

Charisma and the words you use are important, but they're not everything. Your body communicates too. The expression on your face, how you stand, where you look – these are your actions. And they can speak loudly enough to be heard. During conversations, put your phone away. This will let you focus on the person you're talking with. Make eye contact occasionally, but don't stare. Uncross your arms. Crossed arms can communicate that you are closed off. Instead, put your hands in your pockets. Watch other people have conversations. Notice what they do. Then be aware of how you hold your body. You can adjust how you move to communicate that you care.

CHAPTER 5

MAKING AND KEEPING FRIENDS

Keep practising your new conversation skills. Those conversations will probably lead to some new acquaintances. And that's great – it's good to be friendly with the people you see every day. But a friend is someone you feel completely comfortable with. And that's a special thing.

Turning an acquaintance into a friend takes time. A friendship develops in stages. It doesn't just happen overnight. Building a friendship is work, but it is also fun. As you get to know someone better, you let that person into your life. This means opening up – telling your friend some personal things. These things include problems, goals and feelings. It's part of getting to know someone well. It shows that you trust that person to keep your secrets.

Opening up to someone can make you feel vulnerable. This can be a little scary at first. You don't know how others will react. But it is an important part of turning an acquaintance into a friend. Ease into opening up by starting small. Just say something kind of personal and see how that person reacts. Talk about a class assignment that is frustrating you or an upcoming sports game you're nervous about. Does your friend seem supportive? Does he tell you something personal too? If that person opens up too, it shows he wants to be a closer friend.

EMPATHY MATTERS

Another part of being a good friend is understanding and considering what others are feeling. This is called empathy. It guides how you act and what you say. An empathetic friend won't just think of himself. He'll consider his friend's feelings before talking. Imagine that your friend's pet guinea pig just died. You probably wouldn't want to tell him all about your new pet snake. It might make him miss his pet and feel sad.

How do you guess someone else's feelings if you don't know what's wrong? Look at her body language. Listen to what she's saying. Do you get the sense that something's wrong? Do you just feel it? That's your intuition. Listen to it. It means you know something's up.

Show your friend that you care. Ask her if everything is okay. She may not want to talk about it or she might share what's going on. Either way, she'll know that you care about her.

LIFE TIP

It's easy to get cross if you think someone is being mean or rude to you. But before you do, practise empathy. You don't know what's happening in that person's life. Try to think of that person's perspective before you act.

>> DO YOU HAVE EMPATHY?

Take this quiz to see how much empathy you have.
1. Your friend is upset she didn't make the gymnastics squad. Seeing her that way makes you feel:
    a) angry
    b) happy
    c) sad
    d) bored

2. It upsets you when people at school make fun of someone's haircut.
    a) never
    b) sometimes
    c) always
    d) rarely

3. When my friends talk to me about their problems, I:
    a) try to change the subject.
    b) stare off into the distance and tune them out.
    c) listen closely, look them in the eyes and ask questions.
    d) start looking at my phone.

4. Pick the answer that's most like you.
    a) I like making people feel annoyed.
    b) I get annoyed when people are having fun.
    c) I like making people feel happy.
    d) I am too busy to worry about other people's feelings.

If you answered all Cs, you have a lot of empathy for others. If you chose a few Cs, or none at all, try to think of some ways you can be more empathetic. If someone talks to you about a problem, imagine what it's like to be that person. Think about the emotions he or she is experiencing. Like most things, learning to have empathy takes time. Try to remind yourself to be more empathetic each time you talk to someone. Slowly, your ability to be empathetic will improve.

ASK FOR HELP

If you believe you're suffering from anxiety, depression or another mental health issue or are the victim of bullying, ask for help. Reach out to a teacher, parent or another trusted adult. Doctors, psychologists and social workers are available to get you the help you need. You can also reach out to one of these organizations below.

Anti-Bullying Alliance
Offering helplines and advice if you are being bullied.
https://www.anti-bullyingalliance.org.uk

Childline
Online or on-the-phone help, whatever your problem.
https://www.childline.org.uk

Samaritans
You can call or email the Samaritans to talk to someone any time of the day or night.
https://www.samaritans.org

Stem4
Helping teens manage anxiety and mental health issues.
https://stem4.org.uk

Young Minds
Leading the fight for a future where all young minds are supported and empowered, whatever the challenges.
https://www.youngminds.org.uk

FIND OUT MORE

My Anxiety Handbook: Getting Back on Track, Sue Knowles, Bridie Gallagher and Phoebe McEwen (Jessica Kingsley Publishers, 2018)

Relationships (Teen Issues), Lori Hile (Raintree, 2013)

Relationships Whiz: Facts and Figures About Families, Friends and Feelings (Girlology), Elizabeth Raum (Raintree, 2019)

The Anxiety Survival Guide for Teens (Instant Help Solutions), Jennifer Shannon (New Harbinger, 2015)

The Mindfulness and Acceptance Workbook for Teen Anxiety, Sheri L. Turrell, Christopher McCurry and Mary Bell (New Harbinger, 2019)

INDEX